Mastering ChatGPT:

Create Highly Effective Prompts, Strategies, and
Best Practices to Go From Novice to Expert

TJ Books

Contents

Chapter One

ChatGPT Explained

Chatgpt, the invention of GPT, is a revolutionary, new technology as well as an AI-driven language model that uses artificial intelligence to create conversations so similar to those of us humans, that it's hard to tell the difference. Thanks to deep learning algorithms, ChatGPT has been trained on a large library of chat logs, granting it the ability to craft natural replies to your questions andprompts instantly.

The good thing about ChatGPT is that it can generate answers just like those made by people. In short, ChatGPT is a powerful, multi-purpose and valuable tool in generating human-like answers in chatbot applications.

Setting Up ChatGPT

Setting up ChatGPT is pretty straightforward. To get started, the first step is to make an account. Using this AI model is free for now, but it may not remain that way in the future. So take advantage of it for free while you still have the opportunity.

Getting ChatGPT up and running is easy. First and foremost, you must register for an account. At the time of this writing using this ChatGPT is free, but recently an option to "Upgrade" has become available, sparking rumors that ChatGPT may not always be free to access. This is why we highly suggest that you take advantage of its free version, and the amazing opportunities it can provide you with while it is still available for all.

Direct ChatGPT link: Chat.openai.com

Chapter Two

How ChatGPT Works

C hatGPT is an AI-powered chatbot with the amazing ability to not only understand a user's messages, but also to reply to the user in a way that truly feels like talking to another person. It accomplishes this by looking at the messages and using its AI capabilities, like its neural networks and context-aware processing, to understand what is being asked. This helps ChatGPT generate the most suitable and appropriate responses, that makes sense to the user. This makes engaging with ChatGPT feel like a natural, unforced and flowing conversation.

In ChatGPT, the user's messages are referred to as "prompts" and the procedure of commanding ChatGPT to perform any task is called "prompting."

Chapter Three

High-Quality Prompts and Great ChatGPT Responses

When it comes to creating high-quality prompts with ChatGPT, you should know a few basics. One of the simplest, yet most impressive things this AI model can do is it can quickly deliver fully fleshed-out responses, based on whatever prompts you choose to feed its system.

A prompt is a piece of text - questions, thoughts, ideas, or phrases - that you give to the model as a starting point for generating text. A prompt can be a short question, or it can be paragraphs in length.

Here is an example of a prompt

User: "In as few words as possible, describe the heart-brain coherence."

ChatGPT will then generate a response such as: "Heart-Brain Coherence refers to the synchronization of the rhythms of the heart and brain, which is associated with improved physical and mental well-being."

Remember that the responses, or output, generated by ChatGPT are just suggestions. You, as the user, ultimately deicide if you want to use its response as it is, or change it.

Another way you can use ChatGPT is to complete a piece of text. For example, you could give the program the beginning of a sentence like, "Today I went to the clothing store and I bought," and the AI model would continue your sentence with something like "pants, a shirt, and shoes."

It's important to take into account that the quality of the responses, or output, you receive from ChatGPT will depend on the quality of the prompt, or input, you provide, as well as the deep learning ChatGPT has undergone.

For instance, if you ask ChatGPT to explain book genres covered in most Grade 5 English classes to you, and then you ask this ChatGPT to explain College level thermodynamics, it may provide you with a reply that does not make sense. Multiple different conversations at once can confuse the AI model.

In other words, this technology is still quite new, and we users are training it each time we use it. Hence, it will not always be perfect, and it can make mistakes. Therefore, in order to avoid errors, and make the most out of ChatGPT while getting the most accurate responses, it is important that you are consistent with your conversations.

Open a new chat for every topic you want to discuss with ChatGPT. As well, be sure to always be thorough with using high-quality, effective prompts. You will learn the proper techniques for crafting high-quality prompts later in this book.

Chapter Four

Crafting High-Quality Prompts

When it comes to interacting with ChatGPT, there are a few practices that you should keep in mind in order to achieve the best results:

1.Create a clear prompt: When you give ChatGPT a prompt, also called an input, make sure it is easy to understand and well-formatted. This will help ChatGPT to understand what you are asking it to do. When it knows exactly what you are asking of it, ChatGPT will generate more accurate and relevant responses. Prompts may include a question, a statement, a text summary, a bulleted outline, or you can request more information about a topic, etc.

2. **Be specific:** The more specific your prompt is, the better the response, also known as the output, will be. For example, instead of writing this prompt: "Tell me about some popular songs." You could write this more specific prompt instead: "What are the top 20 most popular songs of all time according to Billboard Hot 100 chart?"

3. **ChatGPT will** then **take your prompt** as input **and generate a well-thought-out response** text as the

output, which is the answer to your question. Evaluate its response, and decide if it is satisfactory.

4. **If you decide you want a longer reply**, or more information from ChatGPT, be sure to **follow up with another question**. Because ChatGPT is a chatbox, you don't have to begin a new chat to make changes or glean more information. Simply continue to chat with the chatbox by asking it following up questions as prompts. The AI model was created to remember what you last said and can build on it. This is what makes the platform feel like you are having a chat with a real person!

Pro Tips:

If you receive a response that you like but find that the output is too short.

Simply tell ChatGPT to "expand" on the prompt you wrote.

- If ChatGPT is generating a response you find to be too long, press the button "stop generating" above the chatbox to end its reply.

- Sometimes ChatGPT can forget to finish an output. Thus, it may stop mid-answer. In this case, simply write "continue" to get it to finish its' reply.

- You can also make the model reword its answers by telling it to "rephrase" its response.

- Using "Act as if" or "Imagine that you are" will cause ChatGPT to generate more unique and tailored responses. Ex. "Act as if you are a secret spy," then ask it to help you find a notorious criminal in a story.

- Be as descriptive as you can. You can start with a prompt and then ask more specific follow-up questions.

- If you get an error message in ChatGPT, which often happens these days as the server is overwhelmed by new users, simply refresh the page.

Chapter Five

Ways You Can Begin Your Prompts

There is no wrong way to begin a conversation with ChatGPT, but if you are entirely new to the AI model, this book has provided some popular ways to get you started. Remember to have a clear and specific goal for each conversation with ChatGPT before you engage with it.

Four simple phrases you can use are the following:

"Generate _____."

"Tell me about _____."

"Imagine that _____."

"Act as if _____."

Commands such as "generate" and "tell me about" are pretty straightforward. So let's expand on the other, lesser-known prompts. Some users have expressed great results when they tell the AI model to "act as if" when sending their prompt.

For instance, you may set up the prompt like this: "Act as if you are a dog trainer. What are some effective ways to get a young puppy to stop wetting the carpet?"

From here, you may be satisfied. But if you are not, you may write an additional prompt to keep the conversation going and glean more information. "What is the best home remedy for dog urine in a carpet?"

The prompt "act as if" can work for nearly any career or industry you can think of.

Another prompt that some users have claimed works very well is similar to "Act as if," but may produce different outcomes and generate interesting and imaginative replies. It goes, "Imagine that..."

Some users have used this prompt to create conversations between fictional characters.

Prompt: "Imagine that you are from the year 2050. What are some scientific achievements that have taken place in this time?"

It may give you the generic output stating that it cannot imagine, nor does it have a sense of time. But it will still give you its best response based on the knowledge it has acquired from its deep learning algorithms. (As well, if you tinker with the questions you ask, you will find you can sometimes get around the generic restrictions.) Asking the AI model a question like this can be useful when crafting stories for example. Imagine all the possibilities it can come up with. (No pun intended)

Chapter Six

Key Elements for Successful Chats with ChatGPT

H ere are key factors that determine a successful conversation with you that stays on track and provides the best answers.

Ask the model clear, precise and specific questions: The more precise and straightforward your prompts are, the easier it will be for ChatGPT to understand the information you are asking for. Thus, it can provide the most exact and appropriate answer.

Keep it on Point: When having a discussion with ChatGPT, it is important to stay focused on one topic or task. Moving away from the subject can make it hard for ChatGPT to understand the context and provide satisfactory answers. Therefore, sticking to the same subject during each chat will ensure its replies are as precise as possible.

Be articulate: Structuring your sentences with correct grammar and using the appropriate words is necessary for ChatGPT to understand your questions and provide you with the correct responses.

Be patient: Sometimes ChatGPT needs a few extra moments to process the data and offer a response, so remain calm if a delay arises.

Provide enough good information: If your question involves a certain situation, provide some extra details to help the model understand the context of your inquiry, input, etc.

Offer specific directions: If you are asking the program to go through a particular process, make sure to include very specific instructions. Adding as many details as possible will help it provide a better response.

Chapter Seven

What Jobs Can ChatGPT Complete For You?

F or many users of this amazing technology, ChatGPT's possibilities feel almost endless. Since its launch, the model is regularly updated with new features, which are helping users to find more and more everyday uses for it. Below are just a few of the tasks this technology is being successfully used to complete.

Business: ChatGPT can complete a variety of business-related tasks, making it a favorite amongst entrepreneurs and corporations alike.

Online education: You can leverage ChatGPT for language learning programs, virtual teachers and tutors.

Social media: This technology can generate content and even create replies to posts on social media platforms like Instagram, Facebook, TikTok, Twitter, etc.

Customer service: It can improve customer service by quickly delivering accurate answers to customer inquiries.

Content creation: ChatGPT can likewise generate articles, stories and blog posts with just a starting idea.

Language translation: It can interpret texts from one language into another, which can be very helpful for language learning and communication.

Chapter Eight

Lesser Known, but Awesome Uses For ChatGPT

ChatGPT users are sharing some amazing and clever ways they are using the technology in their businesses, education and even their daily lives. We have included some of the most interesting ones we have heard so far.

Brand Creation (brand bible, brand strategy)

1. Coding for Websites (including taking code from someone's

website and rewriting it for you)

2. Chatbot and Virtual Assistant Responses

3. Content Calendars

4. Contracts

5. Clears Art Blocks (for artists, programmers and writers)

6. Email Campaigns and Drip Sequences

7. Employee Handbooks

8. Essay feedback for school, etc

9. Explanations (can simplify difficult concepts)

10. Financial Reports

23. Outlines (bulleted outlines of transcripts, books just based on the title and author names, articles, podcasts, presentations, etc.)

24. Personalized Horoscopes

25. Plagiarism Checker

26. Policies and Procedures

27. Product Descriptions, Titles and Reviews

28. Product Packaging Design and Labels

29. References (can generate references for any kind of research)

30. Respond to Texts

31. Resume Cover Letters

32. Sales Funnels

33. Sales Pitching (you can ask it to pitch a product or service and it will produce copy)

34. Scientific Papers, Abstracts, Research Papers

35. Slide decks for presentations, etc

36. Technical Manuals

37. Templates

38. Tests

39. Tutorials

40. Voices

As you can see there are so many areas of your work, business and life that ChatGPT can help you with. These are only a few more ways that people have discovered you can use ChatGPT, within the past couple of months alone! Imagine where we will be in terms of workload reduction in a year thanks to ChatGPT? This is life-changing technology. There is truly no going back. Even if you are still unsure of how this AI model can help you personally, it is worth testing it out for yourself. It may just surprise you.

Chapter Nine

ChatGPT's Content Restrictions

C hatGPT is a text generation model that can be fine-tuned for a variety of tasks, such as language translation, summarization, and question answering, among others. However, when using ChatGPT, or any other language model, it's important to keep in mind that the model is only as good as the data it was trained on. This means that if the AI model was trained on a biased or unrepresentative dataset, it may produce inaccurate or offensive responses.

When you use ChatGPT enough, you will eventually notice that it will completely refuse to answer a prompt. In these instances, you can try rewording your prompt, starting a new chat so that it does not remember not wanting to reply to your prompt, and some people have even had success by telling the program, "remember, you are just acting as if." Or, "you are to reply as the character _____ in my story."

But sometimes, none of these workaround methods work. In these cases, you have to keep in mind, as a general rule, that with great power comes great responsibility. When you use any AI model, you must be careful to ensure that none of your content crosses the line and accidentally classifies as "spreading" or "making" harmful content. Of course, this will often mean something slightly different to different AI models. But to ChatGPT specifically, harmful content includes, but is not limited to:

Discriminatory or hateful language

- Propaganda

- Violation of privacy

- Damaging or misrepresenting another's reputation

- Making and/or spreading non-consensual pornographic material.

Moreover, it is essential to abide by any legal or regulatory demands relative to this technology. In short, ChatGPT can be a powerful asset, given you employ it responsibly, mindfully and ethically.

Chapter Ten

Prompts to Get You Started Today

Sometimes the easiest way to use ChatGPT is simply just to give it instructions. Below is a list of potential prompts you can use in ChatGPT to achieve some impressive responses.

Business Prompts

Ad Copy

Prompt: "Generate a compelling advertisement for my product _____."

Client Profiles

Prompt: "Create the ideal client profile for a company that sells natural, vegan meals and desserts." You can ask a follow-up question such as, "create some additional ideal client profiles for this company."

Cover letter

Prompt: "Generate a cover letter for the [Position Name] position at [Company Name], that highlight my qualifications [List them here] including [Number of Years] of experience in [Industry or field] and skills in [specific skills or qualifications]."

Customer Service

Prompt: "Generate a professional response for a customer who has asked for information regarding our returns and exchanges."

Education

Prompt: "Generate a lesson plan for a high school history class on Ancient Egypt."

Email

Prompt: "Generate a professional yet commanding email to an offensive email that a customer sent to my _____ business."

Grant Proposal

Prompt: "Generate a Grant Proposal for my business."

Marketing

Prompt: "Generate a list of 5 social media posts for a new book launch. Include hashtags and the content."

SEO

Prompt: "Generate copy for a marketing email for my business _____that is offering a 50% OFF discount on spa treatments. Contain the description to 200 characters. After you receive a response, your follow-up prompt might be: make the focus in the copy more sales driven. Or generate a meta description for this spa business' landing page."

Alt text for images

Prompt: "Generate alt text for this landing page this is an image of a woman getting laser hair removal on her legs."

Relationships and Messaging

Dating Coach

Prompt: "I want you to act as a dating coach. I will provide a few details regarding a couple experiencing a conflict. Your task will be to provide effective and reasonable advice to help them resolve their issues. Relationship techniques, strategies, and exercises are all welcome. My first question is, "I always end up being the one who remembers important dates, like birthdays and anniversaries. Sometimes I feel like our relationship means more to me."

Messaging

Some users have revealed that ChatGPT has even helped them generate effective and engaging responses to flirty messages on dating apps, texts, etc. But we must warn you to be careful when using it for this purpose, the AI model is picky with the words that are acceptable. For instance, you cannot outright tell it to "flirt" with you.

Prompt: "Act as if you are a charming person. Generate a charming and intriguing response to this message "you look great, how are you?"

Using words like "charming" or "intriguing" bypassed the model's reluctance to engage in outright "flirty" conversation.

Food Prepping and Planning

Meal Plans

Prompt: "Create a healthy, vegan 7-day meal plan. (Once generated, it is recommended that you go through each meal, and tailor the plan to your tastes by eliminating the meals you do not like.) You can include further instructions like, "generate this list again but do not include soy-based foods." Or, "do not include meals that contain bread." You can then tell the program, "generate a list of ingredients I will need for this 7-day meal plan."

And just like that, you will have a meal plan and an ingredient list for each meal. You can also ask it to provide a recipe once you are ready to start making your meals. Finally, "organize this list by shopping aisle."

Recipes

Prompt: "Generate a recipe for a vegan-friendly Thai fried rice that serves

4-8 people. The recipe must include an ingredient list, step-by-step instructions, and approximate prep and cooking times. Do not include soy-based food in this recipe or mushrooms. The recipe should taste flavorful and delicious."

Fundraisers

Prompt: "Generate a professional appeal for a fundraiser." (This prompt can be edited to generate emails, proposals, etc.)

Learning

Explanation

Prompt: "Explain [enter concept] to me like I am a 5th grader."

Essay Feedback

Prompt: "Give me feedback on this university essay about _____."

Language Learning

Prompt: "Act as if you are my Korean teacher and have a class with me for the day." Ask it follow-up questions like, "is this correct?" Or, "provide me with 5

common phrases in Korean that are used while shopping. Use formal Korean."

Lesson Planning

Prompt: "Generate a lesson plan for a 3rd-grade science class."

Translation

Prompt: "Generate a translation of the following text from English to French: 'The hot, bright sun creates summer fun.'"

Research

Prompt: "Generate a summary of the main points in the following research paper: The Impact of TikTok on Children.'"

Transcript and Podcast Summaries

Prompt: "Generate a one-page bullet point form version of the following transcript, using only the most important points." Remember to copy and paste the transcript into the chatbox.

Tutorials

Prompt: "Generate an algebra tutorial and explain it like you are talking to a 6th-grader." A follow-up prompt might be, "give me a list of the most important terms one needs to learn algebra and provide the definition of each."

Motivational Coach

Prompt: "Act as if you are a motivational coach or speaker. When I give you details regarding personal struggles or those of someone else you will provide encouraging affirmations and practical strategies to help the individual develop a better mindset to reach their goals. Here is my first request, I need help feeling motivated about my life considering the state of world affairs."

Social Media

Sponsorship

Prompt: "Generate an email to get a social media sponsorship." Edit and tailor the end result to your liking.

Titles and Topics

Prompt #1: "Generate a clickbait title for a Youtudeo about _____."

Prompt #2: "Generate a viral topic for a Youtube video."

Writing

Creative Writing

Prompt: "Generate a short story about some friends who go to the movies and find out the monster in the film has jumped out of the screen!"

News Writing

Prompt: "Generate a news article about a major historical discovery that has occurred in Asia."

Scriptwriting

Prompt: "Generate a script for a short film about a hunter who sets out on a hunting trip and encounters a sasquatch."

Prompt #2: "Generate this story to read as 1st person, present."

Songwriting

Prompt: "Generate the lyrics for a song about moving on from a bad relationship."

Titles for Books, Essays, Blog posts, etc.

Prompt: "Generate a catchy, four-word title for a book about a child who befriends a talking bear in the woods."

Chapter Eleven

Using ChatGPT Safely and Protecting Your Data

C hecking For Plagiarism

When people think about using ChatGPT safely, plagiarism checks do not often come to mind. But they should. After all, there's always a chance, no matter how small, that the AI model may accidentally generate a response that contains copyrighted information. You do not want to run into unnecessary legal trouble. That is why it is highly recommended that you **always double-check the responses** from ChatGPT **to ensure the information is factual**, and that it is original. This is especially true for any work you plan to publish, profit from, etc.

Two websites you can use include:

Originality AI, is a platform that prides itself as a plagiarism checker and AI detector built for serious content creators. https://originality.ai/

Another great option is the tried and true favorite, Grammarly.

Avoid Submitting Original Content

It's important to remember that ChatGPT is open source, and it does not only provide content to its users, it sources content from its users as well. This is why it is imperative that you **never give ChatGPT your personal information**, and **don't submit full, complete documents that you own as prompts**. This means, do not upload whole stories, business plans, etc, or it is at risk of being used as a source for another user in the future, compromising your copyright, and your ideas.

Use ChatGPT for data, but do not become it.

Saving Your Work

Protecting your data does not only entail not submitting your original works and private data into the chatbox. It also means protecting any information

ChatGPT generates for you. You will find your previous "chats" with the AI model are located on the left sidebar of the program. However, it is highly advised that you back up your important chatlogs onto your computer or into a program like Google Docs. This is because the platform is not perfect yet, and people have experienced entire chat logs permanently disappearing, which has cost them tons of information and work. You want to avoid things like this that waste your time and can cause frustration.

Here are two ways to save your data:

Copy the text from your chatbox window, and paste it into a writing program of your choosing. Save the file to your computer, Google Docs, email, or cloud storage.

2. **Screenshot your chat conversations** if you are using a computer using the PrintScreen button on your keyboard. It will then save as an image on your computer. You can also use your phone to take a photo of your chatlog, and it will save to your device. From there, you can send it to your computer via email, Google Docs, or cloud
storage.

Chapter Twelve

What to Do If ChatGPT Gives You Incorrect Information

It cannot be stressed enough that this AI model is trained on the dataset of millions of websites and content that has come from all over the internet. The information ChatGPT provides is generally correct, but this is not always true. ChatGPT is incapable of verifying the information it generates, which means that sometimes the information it provides is either false, inaccurate, or outdated.

This chatbot is a deep, machine-learning model that is being trained by its users, as much as by web pages, and documents. It can certainly make mistakes, in fact, I have experienced this first-hand. That is why it is so important that you, as the user, cross-check the information it generates for you, with reputable sources in order to make sure the information you are receiving is accurate.

Anytime you discover that ChatGPT has provided you with a response that is not factual, that is outdated, etc. kindly let the AI model know! All you need to do is write it in the chatbox. It will thank you, and the new information you provide will be used to improve its outputs in future updates.

Chapter Thirteen

Making the Most of ChatGPT

As simple as it may seem to use, ChatGPT can be a little overwhelming or even frustrating when you are brand new to the program. Do not give up. Ask it questions you already know the answers to. Ask random, silly questions. Ask pressing questions. Ask ChatGPT to perform tasks you randomly think of and see what happens. Get comfortable using it. The important thing is to remember that the only way to get used to the technology, and generate better and better responses is to practice! As well, join online groups on platforms like **r/ChatGPT** on Reddit, where users are regularly uncovering new ways to use this chatbox.

Like any new application, you will become more familiar with its capabilities and achieve better responses from ChatGPT over time, with patience, practice, research and experimenting with prompts.

Stay curious and creative. ChatGPT is truly at the head of the digital renaissance. When used wisely and responsibly it has the power to save you money, create more time freedom for you, and help take you closer to your dream life.

It's no coincidence that you picked up this book. You have an innovative mind to take an interest in a society-changing technology like this. By taking the initiative to learn this technology, you are setting yourself up to not only become a thought leader in your industry, but studies show early adopters of technology tend to enjoy a larger market share and twice as much revenue as their "technology follower" counterparts.

In short, you are on the right track. Now go out there and craft some amazing prompts!

For More Information on AI, Passive Income, Manifestation, Mindset and More: Follow us

online!https://linktr.ee/DestinyManifest
e

Sincerely,

Destiny Manifeste

Author's Notes

Thank you for reading. If you enjoyed the story or have encouraging or constructive comments please leave a review! It also helps more readers discover my work, so thank you in advance!

Destiny Manifeste was created by two siblings, Jae and Tee. Our aim is to help you recognize and use your divine power to create your dream life! We believe that a happy life is a balanced one, meaning you address and grow in all areas of life: manifestation, mindset, relationships and of course, financial freedom!

We help you address these areas of life through affirmations, mindset development, Law of Attraction techniques, scripting and building businesses that create cash flow/passive income streams that free up your time. Whatever your goals are, we are here to help you learn to manifest using guides, tutorials, and personal coaching.

We also occasionally discuss hidden history, the esoteric and forbidden truths in our decoding videos and podcasts. So be on the lookout for that content as well! If you enjoy content like this, please take a moment to follow us. You are appreciated!

Subscribe to our Youtube channel: https://www.youtube.com/channel/UC0 dkisdT8U4a9YXGLZw4k6A

Follow us on Tiktok: https://www.tiktok.com/@destinymanif este

Listen to our Podcast: https://open.spotify.com/show/4aISdC WFIpfnWyKLtgvqd6

PUBLISH PAGES (Earn Passive income with Self-Publishing):

https://destinymanifest.gumroad.com/l
/

www.ingramcontent.com/pod-product-compliance
Lightning Source LLC
LaVergne TN
LVHW011803070326
832902LV00031B/4651